Designing cars

Designers found that the shape of a car is very important. That is why most racing cars today have a different shape to family cars. They have a slim, smooth body. This helps them to slip through the air as fast as possible. They use materials like **carbon fibre** to make them very light and also very strong.

Waving a chequered flag like this marks the end of a race.

Every sport has rules. In motor-racing, the rules say how big and heavy the cars can be. They also say what engines they are allowed to have.

The world's best racing cars

The most advanced racing cars are **Formula 1** cars.
They need lots of power to go fast and pass other cars.
They also need lots of grip to stay on the track as they
go round turns.

Back to front

Formula 1 racing cars have just one seat for the driver.
The car's **engine** is in the middle, behind the driver.
That means the front of the car can be very low and
slim. This helps it to slip through the air faster.

About 20 Formula 1 racing cars
race against each other in
every race. They race on tracks
all round the world.

Wings for grip

Formula 1 cars have wings on their nose and tail. A plane's wings lift it up into the air. A racing car's wings are upside down, so they push it downwards. This presses the car's **tyres** down hard onto the ground. The tyres grip the road better. The car can then go round corners faster.

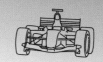

Formula 1 racing car

Engine size:	3 litres/183 cu in
Engine power:	860 horsepower
Top speed:	350 kph/220 mph

television camera

rear wing

cockpit

front wing

engine

engine air intake

A Formula 1 racing car is very fast because it is light and has a powerful engine and a special shape.

Formula 1 cars can be refuelled and have all four wheels changed in less than eight seconds!

Single-seat racing cars

Formula 1 cars are not the only single-seat racing cars. American **Champ Cars** and **Indy Racing League** cars are **single seaters** too.

Champ Cars

Champ Cars are even faster than Formula 1 cars. They have a top speed of almost 345 kph (215 mph). They look like Formula 1 cars, but there are differences. Most racing car engines burn **petrol**. Champ Cars burn a different fuel, called **methanol**. Champ Cars also have wings, but these are different too. That's because Champ Cars race on straighter, faster tracks.

Wings help to give cars more grip on the track.

In dry weather, Champ Cars and Indy Racing League cars use smooth tyres called slicks.

*This is a Champ Car. Champ Cars can **accelerate** from a standing start to 160 kph (100 mph) in about 4 seconds!*

Why do some racing cars use methanol fuel?

Single-seat racing cars in the United States used to burn petrol. They switched to methanol in the 1960s. This is because methanol doesn't catch fire as easily as petrol. Also, if methanol does catch fire, the fire can be put out with water. A petrol fire cannot be put out with water.

Indy Racing

Indy Racing League cars have bigger engines than Champ Cars. But they are simpler, less powerful engines. Like Champ Cars, they use methanol fuel. They race very fast on oval tracks. These have banked (tilted) turns.

These Indy Racing League cars are racing on an oval track.

The fastest racing cars

The fastest cars that race against each other are called **dragsters**. Dragsters race two at a time, side by side. They race along a straight track. This is only 400 metres (a quarter of a mile) long. The cars can reach top speed extremely quickly. But they are not good at turning. They would not go very fast around a race track with bends.

The driver of a Top Fuel dragster sits in front of the engine. The engine is as powerful as eight Formula 1 racing cars!

engine

Car classes

Dragsters are divided into classes. Each class has its own rules. The fastest are the Top Fuel dragsters.

A Top Fuel dragster is a long thin car with an enormous engine. The engine burns a fuel called **nitromethane** and drives giant back wheels. The tyres are made from a soft rubber. This means that they grip the road well. But soft rubber tyres wear out quickly. The tyres of a Top Fuel dragster last for only about six races – that's less than three kilometres (two miles)!

> Top Fuel dragsters accelerate faster than any other racing cars. They can reach 160 kph (100 mph) in less than one second and 530 kph (330 mph) in less than five seconds!

Top Fuel dragster

Length:	**7.6 m/25 feet**
Engine:	**8 litres/500 cu in**
Power:	**7,000 horsepower**
Top speed:	**540 kph/335 mph**

Other dragsters

Top Fuel cars are the fastest dragsters. The next fastest are the strange-looking Funny Cars and the Top Alcohol dragsters.

Funny Cars

Funny Cars look a bit like ordinary cars. Their body looks normal. But look more closely. The body is specially made for the car. It isn't exactly the same shape as a family car. Also, it's tipped up at the back over the big back wheels. The fastest Funny Cars are almost as fast as Top Fuel dragsters.

A Top Fuel Funny Car can accelerate away from the start line as fast as a Space Shuttle being launched.

Normal brakes do not slow dragsters down enough, so they use parachutes! At the end of a race, a parachute pops out from the back of the car. It catches the air and slows the car down.

Methanol monsters

Top Alcohol dragsters look like Top Fuel dragsters, but their engines burn methanol. Methanol is not as explosive as the nitromethane used by Top Fuel cars. This means that their engines are less powerful. But they can still reach a top speed of more than 400 kph (250 mph).

A Top Alcohol dragster can finish a race in just over five seconds.

	Top Fuel Funny Car	**Top Alcohol dragster**
Engine:	8 litres/500 cu in	7.6 litres/466 cu in
Power:	7,000 horsepower	3,000 horsepower
Top speed:	535 kph/333 mph	420 kph/260 mph

The fastest car on Earth

The land speed record is the fastest speed reached by any car on Earth. A car is driven along a straight course about 21 km (13 miles) long. The time it takes to travel exactly 1.6 km (one mile) in the middle of the course is measured. Then the car has to turn round and come back within one hour. These times are used to work out the car's average speed.

Andy Green, the driver of Thrust SSC, sat in a cockpit between the car's two jet engines.

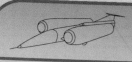

Thrust SSC

Length:	16.5 m/54 feet
Weight:	10,700 kg/23,590 lb
Engines:	2 x Rolls-Royce Spey jets
Power:	100,000 horsepower
Record speed:	1,227.98 kph/763.03 mph

The jet engines of Thrust SSC were made for the F-4 Phantom fighter-plane.

Setting the record

On 15 October 1997, a car called Thrust SSC set a land speed record of 1,227.98 kph (763.03 mph) in the Black Rock Desert in Nevada, in the United States. This was a very special land speed record. It was the first land speed record faster than the **speed of sound**. Thrust SSC had two **jet engines** from fighter-planes. Together, they were as powerful as about 116 Formula 1 racing cars!

As the Thrust SSC raced through the desert, it pushed a wave of air along in front of the car. The air stirred up the sandy ground.

15

Other land speed record cars

One of the most famous land speed record cars was called Bluebird CN7. It was one of the first cars to have a **gas turbine engine**. A gas turbine works like a jet engine.

On 17 July 1964, Donald Campbell took his Bluebird CN7 to Australia. There he set a new land speed record of 648 kph (403 mph).

tail fin

Bluebird's tail fin helped to keep it going in a straight line.

Spirit of America – Sonic Arrow is nearly ten times as powerful as Bluebird, the land speed record car of Donald Campbell.

Sonic Arrow

In the 1990s, a car called Spirit of America – Sonic Arrow tried to set the first **supersonic** land speed record. The driver, Craig Breedlove, sat inside the nose of the car. Behind him was the jet engine of a fighter plane. In 1996, Sonic Arrow suffered the fastest ever car accident. It tipped over on its side at 1,090 kph (677 mph)!

	Bluebird Proteus	Spirit of America – Sonic Arrow
Date:	1964	1996
Length:	9.1 m/30 ft	14.3 m/47 ft
Engine:	Bristol Siddeley Proteus jet	General Electric J-79 jet
Power:	5,000 horsepower	48,000 horsepower
Top speed:	648.7 kph/403.1 mph	1,090 kph/677 mph

The fastest two-seaters

Sports cars are small, light, two-seater cars. They are great fun to drive. Sports cars take part in motor-racing. Some sports cars are almost the same as ordinary cars that drive on the road. Others are specially built for racing.

Built to win

One of the most famous racing sports cars was the Ford GT40. It was built in the 1960s to win the Le Mans 24-hour race. This is a race for sports cars that lasts 24 hours. It takes place near the French town of Le Mans. The Ford GT40 won in 1966, 1968, and 1969.

Racing goes on all through the night at Le Mans.

The Ford GT40 was called the GT40 because it was only 40 inches (102 centimetres) high.

Sports racers today

Modern sports racers have a wing at the back. This pushes the back wheels down so they grip better. Many of them have an open cockpit. One of the most successful sports racing cars today is the Audi R8. An Audi R8 won the Le Mans 24-hour race in 2000, 2001, 2002, 2004, and 2005.

The Audi R8 is typical of sports racing cars today.

Ford GT40	**Audi R8**
Produced: **1966**	**2004**
Engine: **7.0 litres/427 cu in**	**3.6 litres/220 cu in**
Power: **485 horsepower**	**610 horsepower**
Top speed: **330 kph/205 mph**	**330 kph/205 mph**

NASCAR racing cars

NASCAR racing is very popular in the USA. The cars that take part are all built by hand to look like ordinary road cars.

A NASCAR car has a steel frame covered with steel sheets. The driver sits inside a strong cage made from steel tubes. It is called a roll cage. The roll cage stops the middle of the car from being crushed in an accident, especially if the car rolls over on its roof.

HEAVYWEIGHT

A NASCAR racing car is much heavier than a single-seat racing car. It is about three times the weight of a Formula 1 car.

windshield

A NASCAR windshield is made from the same material as the cockpit canopy of a fighter-plane.

A NASCAR car's seat wraps around the sides of the driver's body. The driver is held tightly in the seat by a belt with five straps, called a harness.

Tracks

NASCAR races are held on two different types of tracks. Different cars are built for the two types of tracks. Some cars are built for short tracks. The cars have to go round tight turns as fast as possible. Some cars are built for longer, straighter tracks. The cars go faster on these tracks.

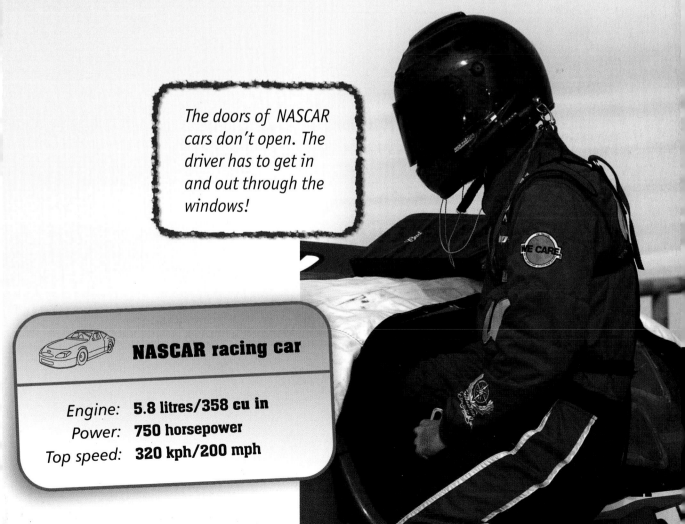

The doors of NASCAR cars don't open. The driver has to get in and out through the windows!

NASCAR racing car

Engine:	5.8 litres/358 cu in
Power:	750 horsepower
Top speed:	320 kph/200 mph

Rally cars

Rallying is one of the hardest types of racing for a driver. Cars set off one at a time and race against the clock. Each rally is actually a series of races called **stages**. One stage might be a muddy track through a forest. Other stages could be icy mountain roads, winding country roads, or loose gravel. There might be 25 stages in a rally.

*Choosing the right tyres for each stage is important. Cars need smooth tyres called slicks for dry roads and grooved tyres for wet roads. They have chunky **treaded** tyres for driving on gravel and special tyres with studs for ice.*

Rally cars have a crew of two, a driver and a co-driver. The co-driver reads a special map. He tells the driver what the road ahead is like.

Rally cars look like ordinary family cars, but they are very different. They are specially built with a more powerful engine and stronger parts. Everything that is not needed is taken out to make them lighter.

Keeping cool

Rally cars are driven as fast as possible all the time. So, a rally car's engine and brakes get very hot. Extra cooling is needed to stop the car from breaking down.

	Peugeot 307cc family car	Peugeot 307 rally car
Length:	4.3 m/14 ft 3 in	4.3 m/14 ft 3 in
Weight:	1,830 kg/4,035 lb	1,230 kg/2,712 lb
Engine:	2 litres/122 cu in	2 litres/122 cu in
Power:	138 horsepower	300 horsepower
Top speed:	208 kph/129 mph	more than 200 kph/ 124 mph

Rally cars are built so that they can be repaired quickly between the stages.

The strangest racers

The strangest racing cars in the world do not have engines! Even stranger, they are powered by sunlight! The cars are covered with **solar cells**. Solar cells change sunlight into electricity. This powers electric motors.

Solar racing

The most important race for solar cars is the World Solar Challenge in Australia. The first race was in 1987. It was won by a car called Sunraycer at a speed of 67 kph (42 mph). In 2003, the race was won by a car called Nuna II at a speed of 97 kph (60 mph).

Solar-powered racing cars are made as low and smooth as possible. This means they slip through the air easily.

The World Solar Challenge race starts in Darwin and finishes in Adelaide. This is a distance of 3,010 kilometres (1,870 miles).

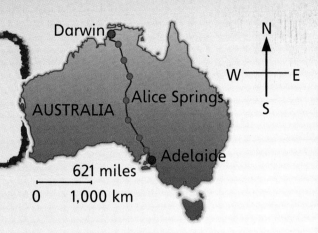

Darwin

AUSTRALIA

Alice Springs

Adelaide

621 miles

0   1,000 km

N
W — E
S

Space car

Nuna II was built with the help of space technology from the European Space Agency (ESA). It was covered with 3,000 solar cells that were originally designed to make electricity for **satellites**. If the solar cells didn't produce enough electricity, the car could also use special batteries. These were made for spacecraft too.

Nuna II's driver looks out through a tiny bubble on top of the flat body.

Nuna II solar-powered racing car

Length:	5 m/16 ft 5 in
Width:	1.8 m/5 ft 11 in
Height:	80 cm/2 ft 8 in
Weight:	250 kg/551 lb
Number of solar cells:	3,000
Top speed:	110 kph/68 mph

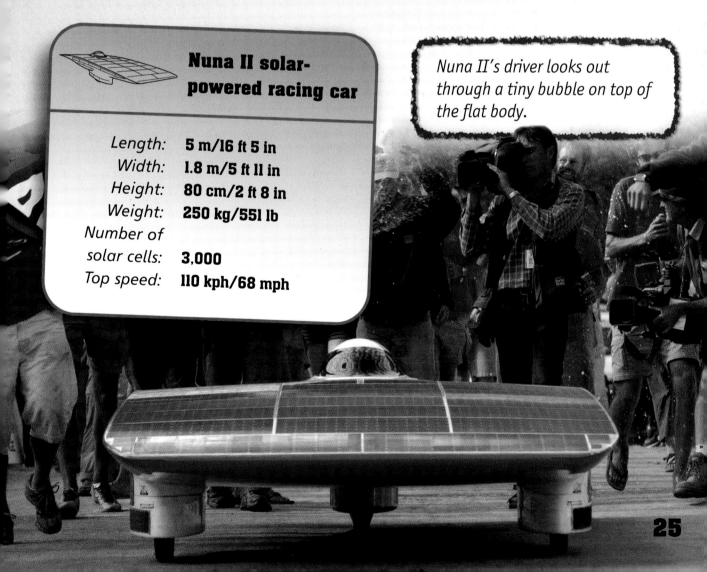

Facts and figures

Some of the fastest, strangest, and record-breaking racing cars are listed here. You can use the information to compare different types of racing cars. If you want to know more about these or other racing cars, look on pages 30 and 31 to find out how to do some research.

Single-seat racing cars	Engine	Horsepower	Top speed	Weight
Champ Car	2.65 litres/162 cu in	750	345 kph/215 mph	710 kg/1,565 lb
Formula 1 racing car	3.0 litres/183 cu in	860	350 kph/220 mph	600 kg/1,323 lb
Indy Racing League car	3.5 litres/213 cu in	700	370 kph/230 mph	703 kg/1,550 lb

Sports and saloon racing cars	Engine	Horsepower	Top speed	Weight
Audi R8 Le Mans sports car	3.6 litres/220 cu in	610	330 kph/205 mph	900 kg/1,985 lb
Ford GT40 Mk II sports car (1966)	7.0 litres/427 cu in	485	330 kph/205 mph	1,111 kg/2,450 lb
NASCAR racing car	5.8 litres/358 cu in	750	320 kph/200 mph	1,545 kg/3,400 lb

Rally cars	Engine	Horsepower	Top speed	Weight
Peugeot 307 rally car	2.0 litres/122 cu in	300	200+ kph/124+ mph	1,230 kg/2,712 lb

Solar powered racing cars	Engine	Horsepower	Top speed	Weight
Nuna II	electric motor	Not known	110 kph/68 mph	250 kg/551 lb

Dragsters	Engine	Horsepower	Top speed	Weight
Top Fuel dragster	8.0 litres/500 cu in	7,000	540 kph/335 mph	1,009 kg/2,225 lb
Top Fuel Funny Car	8.0 litres/500 cu in	7,000	535 kph/333 mph	1,088 kg/2,400 lb
Top Alcohol Dragster	7.6 litres/466 cu in	3,000	420 kph/260 mph	918 kg/2,025 lb

Land speed record cars	Engine	Horsepower	Top speed	Weight
Bluebird Proteus (1964)	Bristol Siddeley proteus gas turbine	5,000	648.7 kph/ 403.1 mph	4,625 kg/9,400 lb
Spirit of America – Sonic Arrow	General Electric J-79 jet	48,000	1,090 kph/ 677 mph	4,570 kg/10,080 lb
Thrust SSC	Two Rolls-Royce Spey jets	100,000	1227.9 kph/ 763 mph	10,700 kg/23,590 lb

Rules and regulations

Racing cars are built according to a set of rules. There are different rules for different types of racing cars. The rules are there to make sure that racing cars are as safe as possible. They also make the cars in each race very alike. This means that races are close and exciting to watch.

Rocket cars

The most powerful engines on Earth are rockets. The most famous rocket-powered car was called Blue Flame. On 23 October 1970, Gary Gabelich drove it to a land speed record of 1,001.6 kph (622.4 mph). Nearly all land speed record cars today are jet-powered. It is easier and cheaper to use old military jet engines and there are lots of people who know how to look after them.

Glossary

accelerate go faster

carbon fibre material used to make parts of some racing cars. It is used because it is light and strong.

Champ Car type of single-seat racing car that takes part in motor-racing in the USA

cockpit the part of a racing car where the driver sits

cu in cubic inch. A space that is one inch long, high, and wide. The space inside an engine where the fuel is burned is sometimes measured in cubic inches (cu in).

dragster type of car used in drag racing

engine the part of a racing car where the fuel is burned

Formula 1 the leading international motor-racing championship. The cars have just one seat, for the driver.

gas turbine an engine that burns fuel to make hot gas. The hot gas hits the angled blades of a turbine and makes it spin. The spinning turbine can drive a car's wheels.

horsepower measurement of how powerful an engine is. Family cars have engines of 50–150 horsepower. Racing cars have 300–900 horsepower engines. Dragsters can have engines up to about 8,000 horsepower. The most powerful land speed record cars have engines up to 100,000 horsepower.

Indy Racing League a type of single-seat motor racing in the United States

jet engine engine that works by burning fuel to produce a jet of gas. Jet engines are also called gas turbines.

methanol type of fuel used by some motor-racing cars

nitromethane very dangerous chemical burned in the engines of the most powerful and fastest dragsters

petrol fuel for car engines, made from oil. Another name for gasoline.

rally motor race which has a series of separate courses called stages. Cars start one after another. At the end of all the stages, their times are added up to work out who has won.

satellite spacecraft circling the world. Satellites make electricity by using solar cells to catch sunlight.

single seater racing car with only one seat

solar cell device that changes sunlight into electricity. Solar-powered racing cars are covered with thousands of solar cells to make electricity for their motors.

speed of sound the speed at which sound travels. At sea level, the speed of sound is about 1,225 kph, but it changes if the air gets warmer or cooler.

stage part of a car rally. The cars set off one after another and they are timed from the start to the finish.

supersonic faster than the speed of sound

tread pattern of grooves cut into a tyre. Tread helps a tyre to grip wet, muddy, or loose ground.

tyre rubber ring around a wheel. Tyres are usually filled with air, but some racing cars fill their tyres with other gases.

Finding out more

You can find out more by looking for other books to read and searching the internet.

Books

Here are some more books about racing cars:

Big Book of Race Cars, by Trevor Lord (Dorling Kindersley, 2001)

Cutaway Book of Racing Cars, by Jon Richards (Franklin Watts, 2003)

Designed for Success – Racing Cars, by Ian Graham (Heinemann Library, 2004)

Monster Machines – Racing Cars, by David Jefferis (Belitha Press, 2002)

Supreme Machines – Racing Cars, by Christopher Maynard (Franklin Watts, 2003)

Racing cars online

These web sites give more information about racing cars:

http://www.discovery.panasonic.co.jp/en/hq/hq07race – this web site for younger readers looks at the Panasonic Toyota Formula 1 racing team.

http://bmw.williamsf1.com – the web site of the BMW Williams Formula 1 team.

http://www.mclaren.co.uk – the official web site of the McLaren Formula 1 team.

http://www.autosport-atlas.com – a web site with news about race cars.

http://www.champcarworldseries.com – the web site of the Champ Car World Series.

http://www.howstuffworks.com/nascar – this web site looks at how NASCAR racing cars work.

http://www.indycar.com – the web site of the Indy Racing League.

http://www.nhra.com – visit this web site to find out all about dragsters.

http://www.wsc.org.au – this web site has information about the World Solar Challenge for solar-powered racing cars.

Racing cars of the past

Famous racing cars of the past include the Mercedes W25 'Silver Arrow' of the 1930s, the Cooper Climax and D-type Jaguar of the 1950s, and the Lotus 78 ground effect car of the 1970s. Can you guess why German racing cars of the 1930s were called Silver Arrows? (Answer on page 32.)

You can find information about record-breaking racing cars and land speed record cars at http://guinnessworldrecords.com.

Index

Answer to question on page 31

Because they were silver in colour. In 1934, the rules said racing cars must not weigh more than 750 kg (1,653 lb)! The new German cars weighed 751 kg (1,655 lb). To make them lighter, their paint was scraped off. This left the silver-coloured aluminium body.

Titles in the *The World's Greatest...* series include:

Hardback   1-844-21262-9

Hardback   1-844-21263-7

Hardback   1-844-21264-5

Hardback   1-844-21265-3

Hardback   1-844-21266-1

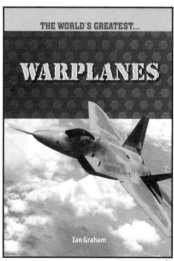

Hardback   1-844-21267-X

Find out about other titles from Raintree on our website www.raintreepublishers.co.uk